Sound not Silence

Nicola Baxter

Watts Books

London ● New York ● Sydney

Sit quietly with your hands over your ears.
What can you hear?

What sounds might you hear in this busy playground?

Almost everything can make sounds.

People can make sounds with their voices.
And they can make sounds in other ways.
They can bang, or blow, or twang.
They can stamp, or clap, or whistle.

Animals can make all kinds of sounds.
They can roar, or squeak, or sing.

Try this later

Make a sound like an animal.
Can everyone guess what animal it is?

Not all sounds are made by living things.
The wind can howl or rustle the leaves.
Raindrops drip and splash.

Now try this
Put your fingers on your throat.
Start to hum.
Can you feel tiny movements?
They are called vibrations.

10

Every noise is made by something moving.
If the vibrations stop, the sound stops.

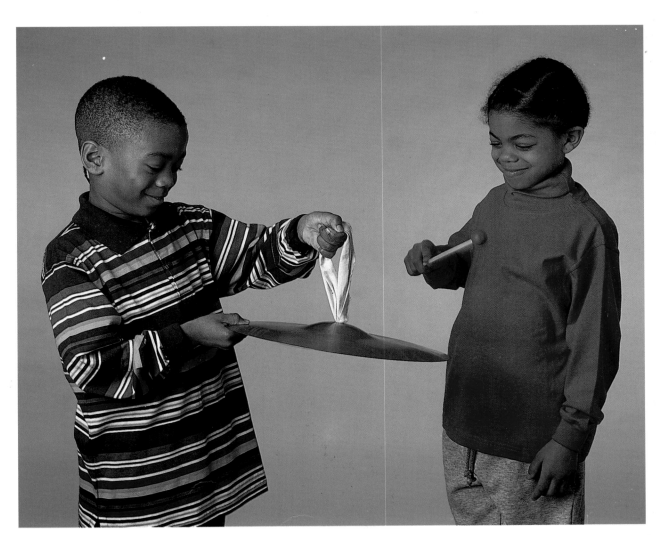

What kinds of movements are making sounds in these pictures?

Sounds move through the air
in tiny waves to reach your ears.

Try this later

Fill a large bowl with water.
Drop a coin or pebble into the middle.
The little waves move outwards
just as sound waves do.

How are sounds different?
Some sounds are soft.
And some sounds are very loud.

We must protect our ears from
very, very loud sounds.

Sounds can be low or high.
They have different pitches.

Try this later

Take two rubber bands and two plastic cartons.
Put the elastic bands round the cartons,
one across and one lengthwise.
Twang the elastic bands.
Which makes the highest sound?

When we talk, we make special sounds.
Other people understand what
the sounds mean.

Sounds in different languages mean
different things.

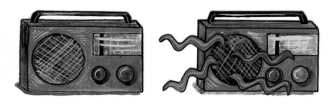

Sit very quietly and listen.
What is the loudest sound you can hear?
What is the softest sound you can hear?
What do the sounds tell you?

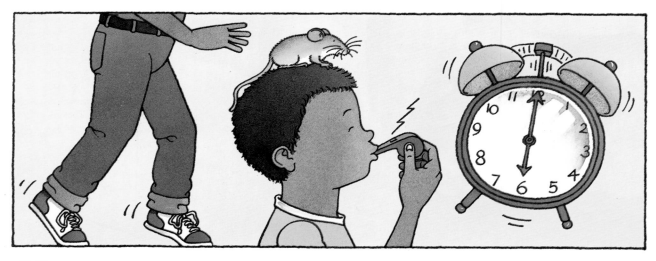

23